Lies we tell our kids

Lies we tell our Kids

Written and Illustrated by
Brett E. Wagner

Lies We Tell Our Kids

Animal Media Group books may be ordered through booksellers, or by contacting:

Animal Media Group
100 1st Ave suite 1100
Pittsburgh, PA 15222
www.animalmediagroup.com
412-566-5656

ISBN: 978-0-9974315-0-6 (pbk)
ISBN: 978-0-9974315-1-3 (ebk)

Author's Note

We've all heard the classic lies that parents tell their kids, and perhaps we've even told some ourselves. "Pick your nose and your finger will get stuck up there!" "Babies get dropped off by storks!"

And while those are fun and strange to a kid in their own right, it got me thinking -- what other fibs would kids believe if they were part of the societal lexicon? Imagine genuinely growing up thinking pincones hatch into gnomes. Or that mallards paint themselves green. Think about the unease you might feel around caviar if you thought the eggs would hatch from inside your stomach!

This book is a collection of these fibs, whether staples of our cultural consciousness or new fabrications, all accompanied by glossy ink drawings.

I hope this book leaves you feeling amused, fuzzy, and a little weird. And I hope you feel nostalgic, whether for falsehoods you believed as a kid, or for an age when you may have bit onto some of these colorful fantasies.

Mittens are made out of recycled kittens.

If you pick your nose,
your finger will
get stuck up there.

If you swallow
mouthwash,
you'll turn teal.

The toothpaste ghost haunts your plaque.

The Police will inspect your toothbrush to make sure you're brushing.

Eat your veggies
or else
they'll eat you.

If you eat caviar, it just may hatch inside you...

and escape.

If you swallow gum,
you'll blow bubbles out
of your butt.

If you don't flush,
a skeleton will rise up from
the toilet and get you.

The finger nail fairy will take your nails if they're not covered at night.

The Monster under your bed just wishes she could read.

If you leave a pinecone around, it will hatch into a gnome.

Stinky feet
breed dragons.

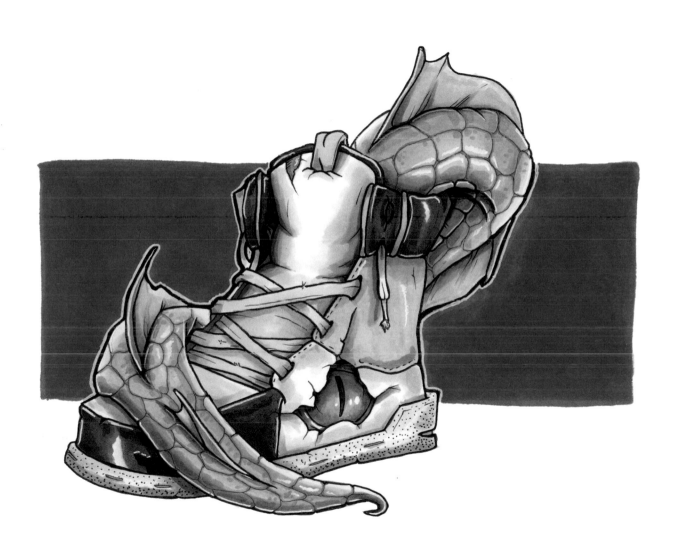

If you cross your eyes, they'll get stuck that way.

One in five avocados have eyes.

Onions make you cry because they're bullies.

Cookies and Cream is made out of bird poop.

Some Coconut trees grow owlets.

Narwhals aren't whales, they're just people with tails.

Dinosaurs went extinct because they couldn't swim.

Islands are whales
who have not yet been
freed.

Fish don't sleep
so that you can.

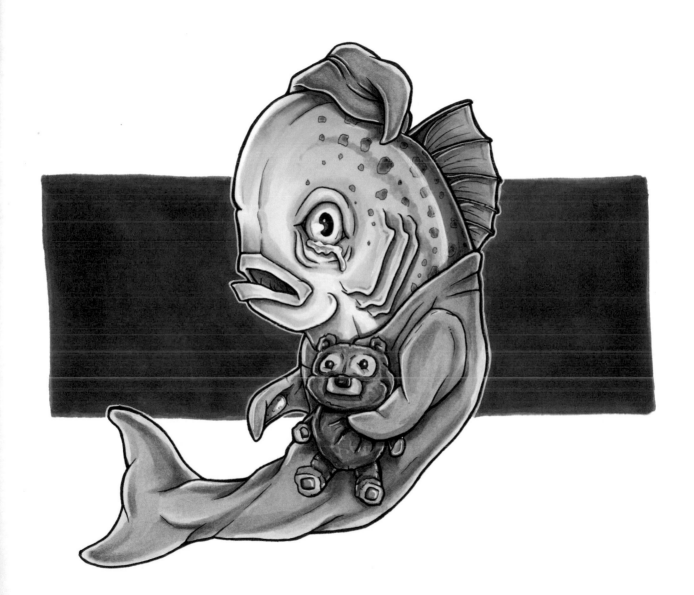

The average spider eats
eight humans a
year in its sleep.

Screech owls don't screech — it's just the sound of the babies they steal.

Storks sell the babies they purchase from screech owls.

Bats are just birds dressed up for Halloween.

Blue Jays are used to give blueberry pie its color.

Toucans
can
can-can.

Mallards paint themselves green at a young age.

Penguins can't fly because they came from space, where they float.

The moon follows your car because it's tied to the door.

Thunder is the sound of angels bowling. Lightning is the flash when they're taking selfies.

Sloths are so slow that they're just now reaching the 1980s.

A rat that eats moldy cheese will grow a second head.

Most rabbits have not developed the taste for flesh... Most.

Most taxidermies are filled with cash — you just need to open them up to find out.

Jackalopes live
in Joshua Tree.

Frostbite

comes from ice cold

wolves.

Don't accept
donuts from gators.

Beavers play hockey with a literal biscuit.

Baboon butts are always sunburned.

The scientific name for dogs is "Woofers", and baby dogs are called "Subwoofers".

Cats with two different-colored eyes have already used up one of their nine lives.

It's illegal for a Koala to work as a banker in Australia.

Seals
love
Clubbing.

Hay bales
are cow
eggs.

Red pandas were
illegal in the 1950s
for fear of communist ties.

FDR once said, "We have nothing to fear but bears by themselves."

Abe Lincoln used a VR headset to simulate the Civil War.

George Washington was the first president to fly in space.